Lighthouse

To Phil & carole,
love from
Abbie x

Lighthouse

ABBIE WIGGINS

LIGHTHOUSE

Copyright © 2024 Abbie Wiggins

All rights reserved. No part of this book may be reproduced or used in any manner without written permission of the copyright owner except for the use of quotations in a book review.

First paperback edition February 2024

Book cover design by Abbie Wiggins & Becky Wiggins

ISBN 9798879199512

@wordsbyabbie on Instagram

To Becky and Sara

Table of Contents

Acknowledgements ix

Preface xi

Part 1 15

Part 2 47

Acknowledgements

Thank you for choosing to pick up this book. Wherever you are and whatever you're going through, I hope that you find light in these pages. I'm glad you're here and I'm thankful for you.

To every person who chooses to follow and share my words on Instagram, I wouldn't be able to do this without you.

    Mum, Dad. Becky, Sara.
    Philbe and Kat.

Preface

After I released my first poetry collection, *Anchor*, I knew I would name my next book Lighthouse. To me, lighthouses are a symbol of hope. I wanted to write something that would show that even in the darkest times, light still exists. I hope that as you read these words, you'll connect with something that points you towards hope and reminds you that you're not alone. Feel free to write, draw or doodle on the pages. I've also made space for notes at the back. This is a safe space for you.

Abbie

When you're in your darkest valley,
when fear grips your heart,
when you're holding it together so tightly,
let these words be a voice of hope,
a flicker of light,
a promise that there is life beyond this darkness
and hope whilst you're in it.

Part 1

ABBIE WIGGINS

The waves
crash over me.

I'm swept away
with the currents,
losing my sense of direction.

Nothing makes sense.

Pieces of me drift away
and I watch them.

How did I end up here?

LIGHTHOUSE

I'm here,
with tears in my eyes,
collecting the pieces.

They won't be swept away.

I'm here.

I don't know
where I am.

I don't know
what to do.

How did I
lose my way?

When did I
drift so far
off course?

Fear fills
my lungs,
it's hard
to breathe.

LIGHTHOUSE

Don't look
at the waves.

Look at me.

We will
guide this boat
to safety together.

I'm frozen,
then I'm burning.

My heart cries out for help,
but I can't speak.

I don't want to swim,
but I definitely
don't want to drown.

So I float,
staring at the sky,
silently screaming for a sign
that things are
going to be okay.

Are things going to be okay?

LIGHTHOUSE

I hear your heart
cry out for help
and I come running.

My hand holds you up
as you float.

It's going to be okay.

The thoughts are
maddening.

I can't ignore them,
but I can't fully let them in.

Time stands still most days.

I'm suspended,
mid-air, waiting for
gravity to take effect.

I can't go back,
but I don't know
how to move forward.

I wait for hope
and long to feel it,
because I know it still exists.

LIGHTHOUSE

You will feel hope again.
You will feel peace again.
You will feel joy again.

I want to be reasonable,
so I reason
and reason
and reason,
until I've convinced myself
that things are okay.

I push my pain
further
and further
and further down,
desperate to
lock it away.

How do you rationalise
something that's not rational?

I try
and try
and try.

LIGHTHOUSE

You don't need
to be reasonable
or rational
here with me.

You can let out
your pain,
we'll unlock it
together.

I close my eyes
so that nothing can
make things darker
but me.

Maybe then I can
fall asleep,
wake up
and pretend it was all
just a bad dream.

But it's real,
so I open my eyes.

LIGHTHOUSE

I know it's scary,
things aren't the way
they used to be
and you wish
you could go back.

I'm holding up a light.

I will help you
through this.

I'd heard stories
of the valley,
but I didn't know
how dark it would be
until I found myself here.

"I can't find the light," I whisper.

My voice echoes.

Fear fills my lungs.

I keep my eyes open.

LIGHTHOUSE

I hear your voice.

I'm still holding up
the light.

We will make it
out of here.

Everything is dark, foggy,
I can't see where I am
or where I'm going.

Fear and despair
hold me captive,
isolated from myself
and those around me.

In the depths,
it feels as if the fog
will never lift,
as if I'll be trapped
here forever.

LIGHTHOUSE

Listen to my voice.

Can you hear it?

This won't last forever.

The fog will lift.

Share your fears with me.

ABBIE WIGGINS

What do you do
when your world goes dark?

Where do you find the light
when it leaves your eyes?

How do you disperse the
thick cloud when it descends?

LIGHTHOUSE

I'll be here when
your world goes dark.

I'll show you rays of light
that will lead you to hope.

I'll sit with you in the clouds
until the sun comes out again.

Waves of fear
catch me off guard
and threaten to drown me if
I don't find a way through them.

The currents pull me
away from the shore
and I don't know how I'll
find a way to safety.

Breathe.

LIGHTHOUSE

Breathe.

We'll find a
way to safety.

There is a way
through the storm.

Breathe.

How do you lean into hope
when things are not okay?

Questions and answers
come to me in waves
and I collect them
like gold dust.

LIGHTHOUSE

This isn't going to be easy.

There will be pain,
there will be loss.

But the truth is
I will sit with you
in your darkest valley
and help you find a way out.

There is more than
what you can see right now.

In the deepest parts
of my heart
I cry out for hope.

I hear a voice,

"Look at me."

LIGHTHOUSE

Look at me.

Can you see me?

Can you hear my voice?

I hear you.

I have so many questions.

What if I can't find a way out?

What if my joy is gone?

What if I feel like this forever?

LIGHTHOUSE

I hear you.

What if we go together?

What if there is more joy for you
than you can imagine right now?

What if I told you
that this is not your whole story?

ABBIE WIGGINS

I believe you.

LIGHTHOUSE

Can you see the lighthouse?

I can see it.

The way to hope
lights up before me.

It's visible.

That's all I need.

LIGHTHOUSE

Let's go.

Part 2

I stand up.

"That's enough,
I'm ready to fight."

LIGHTHOUSE

I'm with you.

I'm holding up
my shield.

We will fight
this battle
together.

I start running.

At first it's slow,
the wind is against me.

It's hard to keep going,
but I'm moving.

That's all that matters.

LIGHTHOUSE

The winds that
try to hold you back
are strong,
but I am stronger.

ABBIE WIGGINS

The shadows behind me flicker
and threaten to steal my focus,
but shadows can only exist
when there is light,
so I keep my eyes
fixed on that light.

LIGHTHOUSE

Keep your eyes fixed on me.

My light shines
even in places where the
darkest shadows live.

I'm here.

ABBIE WIGGINS

Waves of fear
crash and
break
against me.

I feel their impact,
but they don't
break me.

LIGHTHOUSE

You are worth
everything to me.

I will be with you
through every
wave of fear.

ABBIE WIGGINS

I lost pieces of me
out at sea.

They drifted away.

I remember watching
them go.

LIGHTHOUSE

Those pieces,
they're not lost.

I collected them,
kept them safe.

But the thing is,
you don't need them
anymore.

I have something better.

I watch as you
take out pieces
from the bag
you're carrying,
holding each one like
it's precious treasure.

You carefully
hand them to me,
one by one.

I look closer
and realise that
these aren't the old pieces,
they're completely new.

I fit them into place
and they
shine like gold.

LIGHTHOUSE

It's time to let the
old pieces go.

Let's do this together.

I hand you the
pieces I'd collected
and together
we let them go,
one by one
and watch as they
float out to sea.

ABBIE WIGGINS

Light fills me
and I hold it close.

It's more than I
knew existed.

It's not cold here anymore.

LIGHTHOUSE

I won't ask you
to hold it together
or keep it in.

I won't dismiss your pain.

I will stand with you.

I will be right here.

ABBIE WIGGINS

I'm ready to cry.

I'm ready to feel.

I'm ready to trust.

I'm ready to let you in.

LIGHTHOUSE

There's nowhere you could go
that would be too far,
nothing you could say that would
make me turn away.

I see you.

I'm here.

I won't leave.

ABBIE WIGGINS

I'm learning that
I matter.

My voice matters.

My heart matters.

My presence matters.

My thoughts matter.

I matter.

LIGHTHOUSE

You matter.

Your voice matters.

Your heart matters.

Your presence matters.

Your thoughts matter.

You matter.

Hope is the voice that
meets you in the storm
and says,

"There is more than
what you can see right now."

Hope holds my heart
when things don't make sense,
because not everything
will make sense and
not everything
can be explained.

But I've found that
hope always exists,
even in the darkest valleys.

Hope is alive in me.

LIGHTHOUSE

There is more for you.

More hope.

More joy.

More peace.

More love.

More kindness.

More belonging.

More freedom.

THE END

NOTES

NOTES

NOTES

NOTES

NOTES

NOTES

NOTES

NOTES

NOTES

NOTES

NOTES

NOTES

NOTES

NOTES

NOTES

NOTES

NOTES

NOTES

NOTES

NOTES

About the Author

Abbie Wiggins was born in 1996 near Cardiff, Wales. She grew up in Holland and France before moving back to the UK with her family in 2015. In 2019, she received a BA (Hons) in English Literature from the University of Brighton. Abbie started posting her writing on Instagram in 2018 with the aim to spread hope through social media.

Instagram: @wordsbyabbie

wordsbyabbie.com

Other works

Anchor